curious about

HAMMERHEAD SHARKS

BY MONIKA DAVIES

AMICUS LEARNING

What are you

curious about?

3

CHAPTER THREE

Life in the Ocean

PAGE

18

Curious About is published by
Amicus Learning, an imprint of Amicus
P.O. Box 227, Mankato, MN 56002
www.amicuspublishing.us

Editor: Ana Brauer
Series Designer: Kathleen Petelinsek
Book Designer and Photo Researcher: Sara Hood

Library of Congress Cataloging-in-Publication Data
Names: Davies, Monika, author.
Title: Curious about hammerhead sharks / by Monika Davies.
Description: Mankato, MN: Amicus Learning, an imprint of Amicus, [2026] | Series: Curious about sharks | Includes bibliographical references and index. | Audience: Ages 6–9 | Audience: Grades 2–3 | Summary: "What is a hammerhead shark's favorite food? Learn about this unique ocean animal in this question-and-answer book for elementary-aged readers. Includes infographics, table of contents, glossary, books and websites for further research, and index"— Provided by publisher.
Identifiers: LCCN 2024048304 (print) | LCCN 2024048305 (ebook) | ISBN 9798892005050 (library binding) | ISBN 9798892005593 (paperback) | ISBN 9798892006132 (ebook)
Subjects: LCSH: Hammerhead sharks—Juvenile literature.
Classification: LCC QL638.95.S7 D38 2026 (print) | LCC QL638.95.S7 (ebook) | DDC 597.3/4—dc23/eng/20241207
LC record available at https://lccn.loc.gov/2024048304
LC ebook record available at https://lccn.loc.gov/2024048305

Photo Credits: Alamy Stock Photo/ArteSub, 3, 18–19, Tobias Friedrich, cover, 1, WaterFrame_fur, 17; Getty Images/by wildestanimal, 15, Colors and shapes of underwater world, 4-5, Gerard Soury, 2, 6, Ken Kiefer 2, 2, 12–13, 9, 10–11, Norbert Probst, 21, Photo by Danny James, 14; Shutterstock/ KS-Design, 7; The Noun Project/Bakunetsu Kaito, 22, 23, Dolly Holmes, 22, supalerk laipawat, 23; Voctoozy/om1947, 8

CHAPTER ONE

Why are they called hammerheads?

Hammerhead sharks have a one-of-a-kind look. Their flat, wide head looks like a hammer or mallet! This makes their name easy to remember. Some hammerheads are gray, while others are brown. Most have white bellies.

DID YOU KNOW?
The largest hammerhead shark weighed almost 1,000 pounds (454 kilograms). A grand piano weighs about the same!

Hammerhead sharks have a lifespan of 20 to 30 years.

A scalloped bonnethead is the smallest hammerhead shark.

Are there different kinds of hammerhead sharks?

COMPARING SIZES: How big is a hammerhead shark?

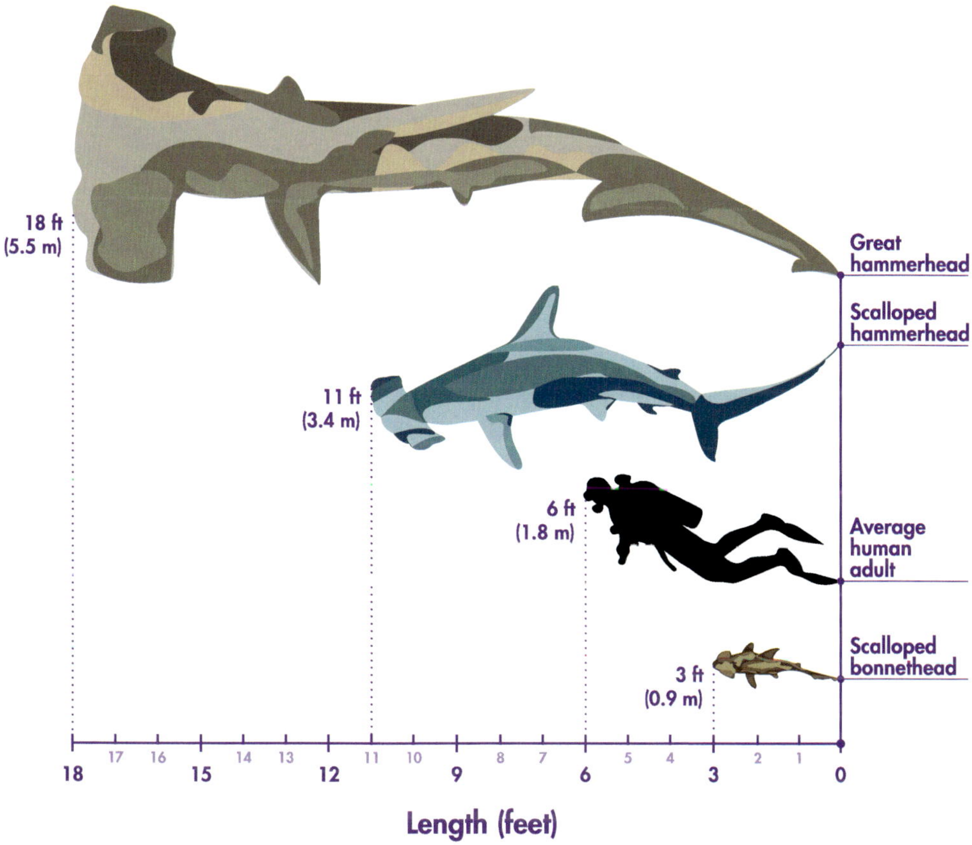

Yes! There are at least nine different **species** of hammerheads. They come in all sizes. The largest is the great hammerhead. The smallest is the scalloped bonnethead. But they all share the same **distinctive** head shape.

Can I swim with one?

You can if you are careful! Hammerheads do not usually attack humans. Their small mouths are better for eating fish. The sharks like to swim in warm waters. They are found in most of our oceans. They usually stay close to land.

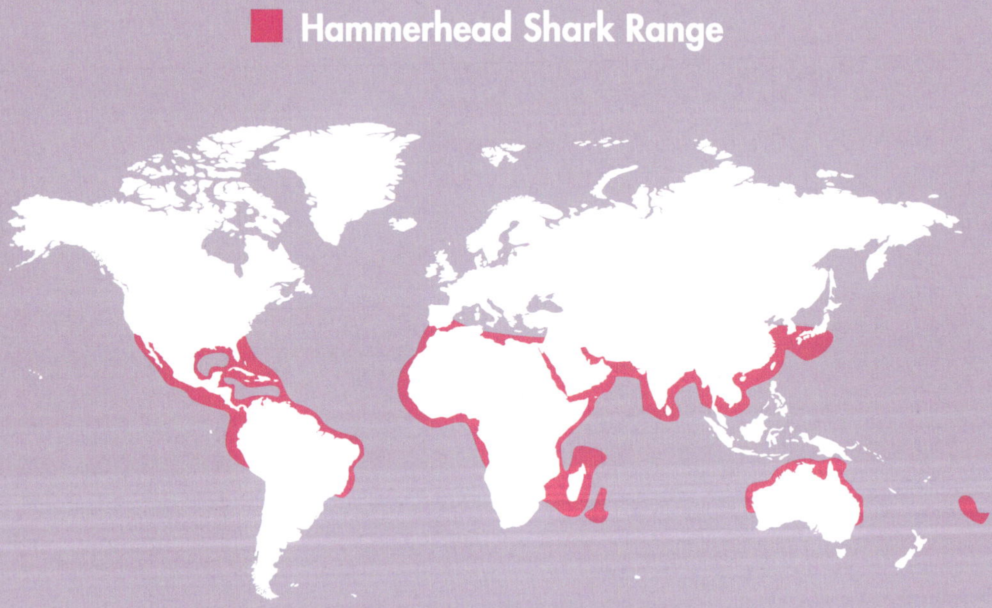

Divers often swim with hammerheads.

Why are their heads shaped like that?

No one is sure! Hammerheads have a single eye and **nostril** on each side of their head. To see, they move their head from side to side. This lets them look around quickly and gives them a 360-degree view.

Every hammerhead has a flat, T-shaped head.

DID YOU KNOW?

There are three hammerhead shapes: smooth, scalloped, and great. Can you tell them apart?

smooth

scalloped

great

CHAPTER TWO

How do hammerhead sharks hunt?

Hammerheads use their wide head to pin **prey** to the ground. They also have special **organs** on their heads. These organs can sense electric fields from other fish. They use this skill to find fish hiding in the sand!

Hammerheads often hunt alone.

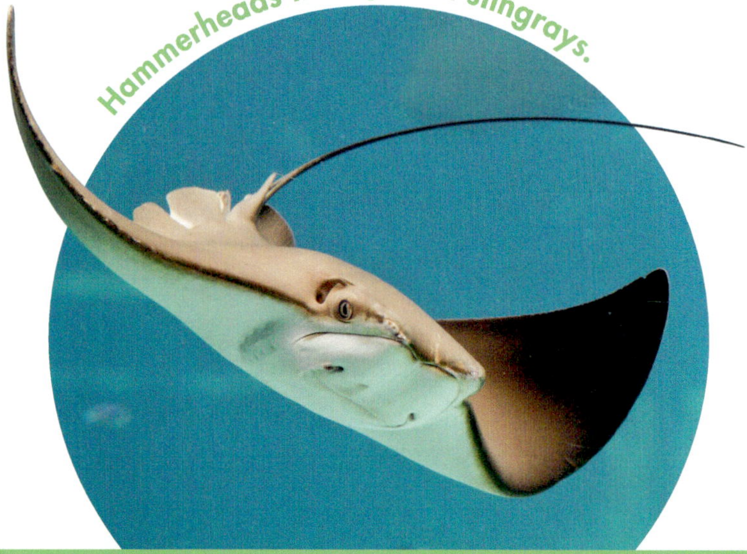

What do hammerheads eat?

It depends on the type of hammerhead. Smaller hammerheads have flatter teeth. They chew on crabs, shrimp, and fish. Larger hammerheads have teeth that cut into their prey. Stingrays are their favorite meal. They also eat squid and other sharks.

A hammerhead will eat anything it can catch.

Do hammerheads swim sideways?

Some of them do! Most sharks have longer fins on their sides. But hammerheads have a taller dorsal fin. These fins are on top of their body. Swimming sideways helps them save **energy**. They also swim faster sideways.

Hammerheads often swim at an angle between 50 and 75 degrees.

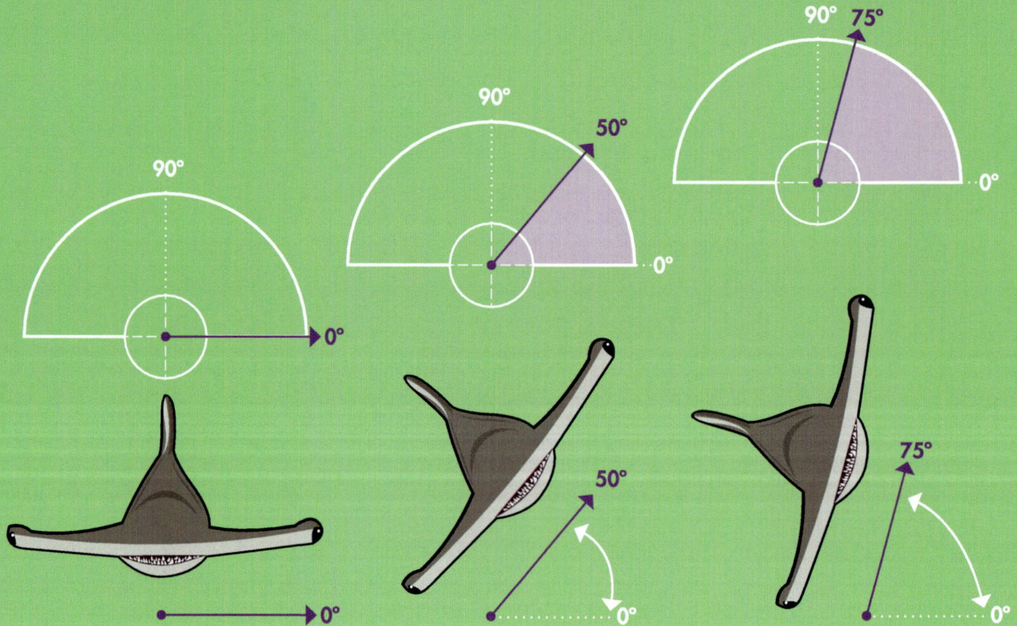

Hammerheads roll over while they swim.

How are hammerhead shark babies born?

Baby hammerheads are called pups.

DID YOU KNOW?
Hammerheads are born with soft heads. That way they do not get stuck during birth.

Hammerhead babies start their lives inside eggs. The eggs **hatch** inside the mother shark after about 11 months. The mothers always give birth to live young. They can have up to 42 babies! The babies are about 2 ft (0.6 m) long.

Are hammerhead sharks endangered?

Scalloped bonnetheads are critically **endangered**. Others are threatened. They are overfished. They can get caught in fishing nets. Some humans hunt them for food. The sharks are also prized for their fins. This unique shark is getting harder to find in our oceans.

DID YOU KNOW?

As of 2024, it is against the law for fishers to keep hammerhead sharks in the US Caribbean.

Scalloped bonnetheads are the most endangered hammerheads.

STAY CURIOUS!

ASK MORE QUESTIONS

Do hammerhead sharks stay in one place?

Where is the best place to see a hammerhead shark?

Try a BIG QUESTION: How can humans take care of hammerhead sharks?

SEARCH FOR ANSWERS

Search the library catalog or the Internet.
A librarian, teacher, or parent can help you.

Using Keywords
Find the looking glass.

Keywords are the most important words in your question.

If you want to know about:

- hammerhead shark movement, type: HAMMERHEAD SHARK MIGRATION
- where to find hammerheads, type: HAMMERHEAD SHARK LOCATIONS

FIND GOOD SOURCES

Here are some good, safe sources you can use in your research.
Your librarian can help you find more.

Books

Hammerhead Shark
by Jenna Lee Gleisner, 2020.

Hammerhead Sharks
by Rebecca Pettiford, 2021.

Internet Sites

Britannica Kids | Hammerhead Shark
https://kids.britannica.com/kids/article/hammerhead-shark/639024
Britannica Kids is full of kid-friendly, fact-checked articles.

National Geographic Kids | Hammerhead Shark
https://kids.nationalgeographic.com/animals/fish/facts/hammerhead-shark
National Geographic Kids is a great source to discover information about animals.

Every effort has been made to ensure that these websites are appropriate for children. However, because of the nature of the Internet, it is impossible to guarantee that these sites will remain active indefinitely or that their contents will not be altered.

SHARE AND TAKE ACTION

Most people think sharks are scary! Hammerhead sharks may be predators, but they usually do not hunt humans.
Share what you have learned with your friends.

The plastic in our oceans hurts sea creatures. Find ways to use less plastic.
Bring a cloth bag for shopping.
Use a reusable water bottle.

Help take care of the oceans for hammerheads.
Join a beach clean-up.
Try to use less water.

GLOSSARY

distinctive Having a feature that makes a thing different than others.

endangered To describe a kind of animal that has become hard to find and could die out completely.

energy Ability to move or be active.

hatch To be born by coming out of an egg.

nostril One of the two nose openings.

organ Part of the body that has a certain function.

prey An animal that is hunted by another animal for food.

species A group of animals that are similar and can make young animals.

INDEX

About the Author

Monika Davies is a Canadian author of over 60 books for young readers. She thinks sharks are fascinating—and hopes you agree! When Monika isn't writing, you can find her strolling by the ocean, reading books too quickly, or trying to keep her seven plants alive.